Navigating Life with Adult ADHD

A Guide on How Adults Can Manage Their Attention Deficit Disorder

Alyssa Hutchens

Table Of Content

INTRODUCTION

In a world buzzing with continual stimuli and demands, keeping concentration and attention may be a tough achievement for anybody. But for adults dealing with Attention Deficit Disorder (ADD), these everyday problems may become much more obvious, impacting numerous facets of their life. If you find yourself battling with inattention, impulsivity, and trouble in organizing chores, you are not alone. This book, "Adults Attention Deficit Disorder," is intended to provide you a path to a more satisfying and productive existence.

Attention Deficit Disorder, popularly known as ADHD, is not a simple lack of attention or a character fault; it is a neurodevelopmental illness that affects millions of people worldwide. While ADHD is commonly associated with children, the fact is that it may continue into maturity, and many people may go misdiagnosed until later in life. If you have recently gotten a diagnosis or have long suspected that you could have ADHD, this book will act as your companion in understanding, managing, and flourishing with this illness.

Chapter by chapter, "Navigating Life with Adult ADHD" will walk you through the process of learning the complexity of adult ADHD and give you practical ideas and ways to confront its obstacles. Together, we will study the complexities of ADHD, separating it from typical distractions and investigating its specific influence on your personal and professional life.

In Chapter 1, we go into the foundations, setting the framework for understanding Adult ADHD. We will discuss the diagnosing process, separating adult symptoms from childhood presentations, and revealing how ADHD may significantly affect your day-to-day life. By the conclusion of this chapter, you will have a firm idea of what

ADHD means for you and how it may be treated.

Chapter 2 is dedicated to arming you with excellent coping skills and practices. Here, you will learn about Cognitive Behavioral Therapy (CBT) and how it may be a useful tool in altering cognitive patterns and regulating impulsive behaviors. We will also dig into the art of time management and organizing, crucial skills for people with ADHD, and introduce mindfulness methods to boost attention and concentration.

In Chapter 3, we discuss the role of medication and lifestyle alterations in ADHD treatment. While medicine is not the sole option, knowing its potential advantages and working in cooperation with healthcare providers may lead to significant gains. Moreover, we highlight the value of adopting a healthy lifestyle, including exercise, diet, and sleep, as these may significantly affect your overall well-being and help alleviate ADHD symptoms.

Throughout this trip, you will be encouraged to establish a solid support system, incorporating loved ones and peers who can give understanding, encouragement, and empathy. We know that living with ADHD is a shared experience, and establishing relationships with others who face similar struggles may be immensely inspiring.

In conclusion, "Navigating Life with Adult ADHD" attempts to equip you with the skills, information, and support you need to manage the complexity of Adult ADHD. It is a monument to the power and perseverance of people like you who accept their unique neurodiversity and aim to unleash their full potential. By learning to adapt, adopting effective tactics, and obtaining the correct assistance, you will begin on a revolutionary path toward mastering attention and reclaiming control of your life.

Always remember, you are not defined by ADHD; instead, you have the freedom to choose your story. Let this book be your guide in exposing the incredible abilities inside you and inspiring you to flourish, not despite ADHD, but alongside it. Let us now begin on this instructive adventure together, as we discover the way to mastering attention and recovering your life.

CHAPTER 1

Understanding Adult ADHD

ADHD and its incidence in adulthood

Adult attention-deficit/hyperactivity disorder (ADHD) is a mental health illness that encompasses a mix of chronic issues, such as trouble paying attention, hyperactivity, and impulsive conduct. Adult ADHD may lead to unstable relationships, poor work or school performance, low self-esteem, and other challenges.

Though it's dubbed adult ADHD, symptoms start in early infancy and persist throughout age. In some cases, ADHD is not noticed or diagnosed until the person is an adult. Adult ADHD symptoms may not be as evident as ADHD symptoms in youngsters. In maturity, hyperactivity may reduce but concerns with impulsiveness, restlessness, and difficulty paying attention may continue.

Prevalence in Adults:

Traditionally, ADHD was assumed to be an illness that mostly affected children and teenagers. However, research over the years has revealed that ADHD may continue into adulthood for a considerable proportion of people. According to the American Psychiatric Association's Diagnostic and Statistical Manual of Mental Disorders (DSM-5), roughly 5% of children and 2.5% of adults worldwide have been diagnosed with ADHD.

It's vital to highlight that the frequency of ADHD in adults may be underestimated owing to numerous reasons:

Underdiagnosis and Misdiagnosis: Many persons with ADHD may go untreated or misdiagnosed until adulthood. This is partially because the symptoms of ADHD in adults might vary from those in children and are typically less overt. Instead of hyperactivity, people with ADHD may suffer inner restlessness or feel a continual sensation of mental activity.

Gender Differences: ADHD is more typically diagnosed in boys throughout childhood. However, in maturity, it is considered that the ratio between men and women with ADHD is more equal. This shows that ADHD could be underdiagnosed in females throughout childhood, leading to fewer recognized instances in adult women.

Stigma and Lack of Awareness: ADHD in adults is still susceptible to social stigma, which may dissuade some persons from obtaining professional care. Additionally, many individuals may not be aware that their challenges in concentration, organization, and impulsivity might be connected to ADHD.

Coping Mechanisms: Over time, some people develop coping mechanisms to manage their ADHD symptoms, making it difficult to diagnose the underlying disease.

There are three key components that makeup ADHD, namely:
- Hyperactivity,
- Inattention,
- Impulsiveness

These three basic symptoms that constitute ADHD may be found in both children and adults, but vary in how they manifest between these two. As a person travels through different
phases of life, you will observe a change in how the symptoms emerge. With youngsters, the symptoms look more evident, however with adults they could be more difficult to identify. As adults have had to live with these symptoms for a much longer period, they're more likely to have learned strategies to cover up their symptoms or create excuses for them. So

it's incredibly crucial to be able to detect and comprehend the distinctions in the ways symptoms of ADHD present in children and adults.

What's average conduct and what's ADHD?

Almost everyone has some symptoms related to ADHD at some time in their life. If your troubles are new or happened only sporadically in the past, you probably don't have ADHD. ADHD is diagnosed only when symptoms are strong enough to create continuing issues in more than one area of your life. These chronic and disruptive symptoms may be traced back to early infancy.

Diagnosis of ADHD in adults may be challenging since many ADHD symptoms are similar to those caused by other diseases, such as anxiety or mood problems. And many individuals with ADHD also have at least one additional mental health disorder, such as sadness or anxiety.

Symptoms of ADHD in Adult

Other folks with ADHD have decreased symptoms as they mature, while other adults continue to have severe symptoms that interfere with normal functioning. In adults, the major characteristics of ADHD may include trouble paying attention, impulsiveness, and restlessness. Symptoms might vary from moderate to severe.

Many folks with ADHD aren't aware they have it - they only know that ordinary chores may be a difficulty. Adults with ADHD may find it difficult to concentrate and prioritize, leading to missed deadlines and forgotten meetings or social activities. The failure to manage emotions may range from dissatisfaction with waiting in line or driving in traffic to mood swings and outbursts of fury.

Adult ADHD symptoms may include:

- Impulsiveness
- Disorganization and issues prioritizing
- Poor time management skills
- Problems focussing on an assignment
- Trouble multitasking
- Excessive activity or restlessness
- Poor planning
- Low frustration tolerance
- Frequent mood swings
- Problems following through and finishing assignments
- Hot temper
- Trouble dealing with stress

The distinction between childhood and adult ADHD symptoms.

The symptoms of Attention Deficit Hyperactivity Disorder (ADHD) range in their appearance between children and adults. In youngsters, the symptoms may be more visible, whereas adults have frequently discovered methods to cover up or create excuses for their problems. It's vital to recognize the distinctions in the ways that ADHD symptoms manifest in children vs adults.

Three key components constitute ADHD: hyperactivity, inattention, and impulsiveness. Not everyone diagnosed with attention deficit disorder has all three.

Hyperactivity

Hyperactivity in youngsters is as though the kid is in continual motion. They may be running, climbing on objects, frequently finding it difficult to sit still, wriggling in the classroom, and continually fidgeting. This continual mobility is above and above typical childhood activity, and despite the child's best efforts, does not appear to be within their self-control.

In adults, hyperactivity is perceived more as a general restlessness, with difficulties sitting still for extended amounts of time (such as in class, at the movies, or at work), and becoming more readily bored with things once learned. They may also feel fidgety, and frequently have an inward sensation of restlessness inside of them. An adult with hyperactivity is constantly on the move and typically doesn't react well to difficult circumstances.

Inattention

The variation in inattention symptoms between children and adults isn't generally as obvious. A person with inattention, whether a kid or adult, may make thoughtless errors, doesn't complete what they start, and may not pay attention to details.

In youngsters, this shows across most clearly in schooling, but may also present itself in chores or projects. Both children and adults may lose or misplace items, particularly crucial things like paper required for school or job, keys, or mobile phones.

In adults, these symptoms appear more around the job and everyday routines of life. For instance, at work, an adult may attempt to move from job to task ("multi-tasking"), but never finish any of them, and so their overall work performance declines.

Impulsiveness

Impulsive children tend to act without thinking through the consequences of their actions (such as jumping off a high place without considering where they may land, such as on someone else standing there) or blurt out an answer before being called on. Impulsivity is more noticeable in children when they skip lines and don't wait their turn.

Adults may similarly blurt out an answer at a business meeting, but their impulsivity also may show through in their spending habits, conversation disruptions, and indulging in unsafe actions, such as driving too fast. They may complete other people's words for them or even dominate a discussion.

Impact on Adults

ADHD, or Attention Deficit Hyperactivity Disorder, may have a substantial influence on individuals in different facets of their life. The obstacles offered by this neurodevelopmental illness may influence personal, academic, and professional arenas, resulting in a variety of problems and hardships. Understanding the effect of ADHD on adults is vital for establishing suitable strategies and therapies to assist them lead satisfying lives.

Work and Career:

- Adults with ADHD may experience difficulty in keeping concentration, retaining attention on activities, and organizing their work. This might lead to issues meeting deadlines and performing work tasks, possibly compromising job performance and career possibilities.

- Impulsivity may lead to quick judgments or improper statements in professional contexts, which may impact working relationships and career chances.
- Adults with ADHD could have problems with time management, making it tough to stick to schedules and perform work effectively.

Education & Learning:
- For people seeking higher education or professional growth, ADHD may provide problems in learning, remembering knowledge, and organizing assignments.
- Adult students with ADHD may struggle to keep organized, manage deadlines, and prioritize tasks, impacting their academic performance and advancement.

Relationships and Social Life:

- The symptoms of ADHD, such as forgetfulness, impulsivity, and trouble listening, may influence personal relationships. Adults with ADHD may have problems sustaining continuous communication and may look inattentive to the demands of their partners, friends, or family members.
- Impulsivity may occasionally lead to impulsive spending, resulting in financial pressure and unhappiness in relationships.

Emotional Well-being:
- Coping with the issues of ADHD may be emotionally exhausting. Adults with ADHD may feel greater stress, dissatisfaction, and a sense of underachievement owing to their challenges in numerous aspects of life.
- Low self-esteem and feelings of inadequacy may occur when persons with ADHD compare themselves to

those who do not suffer comparable challenges.

Health and Safety:
- Impulsivity and distractibility may occasionally lead to accidents or unsafe activities, jeopardizing personal safety.
- Difficulties with organization and time management may impair health-related behaviors, such as exercise, eating, and obtaining appropriate sleep.

Long-Term Outcomes:
- Without adequate care and assistance, untreated ADHD may have long-term implications for an individual's personal and professional development, possibly leading to difficulty in fulfilling life goals and objectives.

Despite the issues ADHD causes, it is crucial to understand that persons with ADHD also possess distinct qualities and abilities. With the correct therapies and support, individuals with ADHD may learn to manage their symptoms successfully, capitalize on their abilities, and discover ways that work for them. Treatment techniques, such as behavioral therapy, medication, and lifestyle improvements, may considerably enhance an adult's capacity to live with ADHD and achieve success in numerous aspects of life.

Support from family, friends, employers, and educators plays a critical part in building a friendly and understanding environment for persons with ADHD. Recognizing and accepting neurodiversity is vital in establishing a culture that appreciates and accommodates persons with ADHD, enabling them to flourish and offer their unique views and abilities to the world.

Common obstacles experienced by individuals with ADHD in numerous parts of life.

Adults with ADHD typically confront several obstacles in several parts of their life. While the particular obstacles may vary from person to person, some frequent challenges experienced by individuals with ADHD include:

Workplace Performance: Adults with ADHD may have difficulty with time management, organization, and meeting deadlines at work. They could find it tough to retain concentrate on tasks, resulting in lower productivity and possibly hurting job growth chances.

Academic Pursuits: For people seeking higher education or professional development, ADHD may provide problems in learning, remembering knowledge, and organizing homework. They may have trouble completing homework and preparing for tests.

Relationships: The symptoms of ADHD, such as forgetfulness, impulsivity, and trouble listening, may influence personal relationships. Adults with ADHD may have problems sustaining continuous communication and may look inattentive to the demands of their partners, friends, or family members.

Financial Management: Impulsivity in spending and difficulties in planning and arranging funds may contribute to financial issues for persons with ADHD.

Time Management: Struggling with time management may influence many parts of an adult's life, from being regularly late for appointments and social occasions to challenges in organizing daily tasks.

Household Organization: Adults with ADHD may have problems arranging their living area and keeping it neat, resulting in clutter and disorder.

Emotional Regulation: Emotional dysregulation is typical in adults with ADHD. They may have heightened emotions, mood fluctuations, and trouble dealing with irritation or stress.

Procrastination: Adults with ADHD may find it tough to undertake activities or initiatives, resulting in procrastination and delays in fulfilling critical obligations.

Impulsive Decision-making: Impulsivity may lead to fast judgments with possible effects on different life elements, such as relationships, money, and professional choices.

Physical Health: Difficulties in maintaining a regular exercise program and sticking to appropriate food habits may influence the physical well-being of persons with ADHD.

Mental Health: Adults with ADHD may be at increased risk for anxiety, depression, and other mental health concerns owing to the persistent stress and difficulty they confront in numerous aspects of life.

Social Skills: ADHD symptoms may influence social relationships, making it hard to establish friendships or engage in social activities.

Driving and Safety: Impulsivity and inattention may impair driving behavior and safety, resulting in an increased risk of accidents.

It's crucial to remember that persons with ADHD also possess distinct abilities and talents. With proper therapies, support, and understanding, people may learn to manage their symptoms successfully and capitalize on their abilities. Behavioral therapy, medication, and lifestyle improvements are some of the ways that may help individuals with ADHD negotiate these problems and lead satisfying lives. Building a supporting network of family, friends, and coworkers who understand ADHD and give encouragement is also vital in conquering these issues.

Diagnosis and Evaluation

For a range of reasons, some individuals aren't diagnosed with the illness when they are young. Getting a correct diagnosis as an adult may be life-changing. When neglected, the illness may create major health, professional, and relationship difficulties.

Can ADHD Symptoms Be Readily Seen?
The key to any effective diagnosis of ADHD is looking at the complete picture since a lot of the symptoms are merely something most people do once in a while. Someone with ADHD, however, does these things all the time, and truly can't prevent themselves from doing them since it's not a conscious decision.

A person with ADHD has symptoms that severely influence their ability to function in two or more separate areas in their life, such as at school and home, or at work and home. Living with untreated ADHD is a daily battle, with the symptoms intensifying during times of stress.

More subtle indicators of ADHD may be observed largely in the inattention component since someone who's not paying attention might be daydreaming as we all do from time to time or actually be suffering with maintaining focus on the meeting or class. A person with ADHD would battle with this inattention almost all the time, in most settings, while a person who doesn't have ADHD will be able to concentrate and pay attention most of the time.

A person with poor self-esteem or anxiety may be suffering from ADHD first and foremost, but instead, the other worry, such as anxiety, is regarded as the fundamental problem, when it's actually simply a symptom. Sometimes someone may be considered as not as brilliant as others then again, they cannot simply concentrate on the work that's hindering their seeming intellectual talents.

Standard therapies for ADHD in adults often entail medication, education, skills training, and psychological therapy. A mix of these is frequently the most effective therapy. These therapies may help control many symptoms of ADHD, but they don't cure it. It may take some time to establish what works best for you.

Medications

Talk with your doctor about the advantages and hazards of any drugs.

- Stimulants, such as medicines that contain methylphenidate or amphetamine, are often the most frequently given treatments for ADHD, however, other medications may be provided. Stimulants seem to enhance and balance levels of brain chemicals called neurotransmitters.

- Other drugs used to treat ADHD include the non-stimulant atomoxetine and some antidepressants such as bupropion. Atomoxetine and antidepressants operate slower than stimulants do, however, they may be effective alternatives if you can't take stimulants because of health concerns or if stimulants create significant negative effects.
- The proper drug and the right dosage differ across people, so it may take time to figure out what's suitable for you. Tell your doctor about any adverse effects.

Psychological counseling

Counseling for adult ADHD often involves psychological counseling (psychotherapy), information about the illness, and learning techniques to help you be successful.

Psychotherapy may help you:

- Improve your time management and organizational skills
- Learn how to lessen your impulsive behavior
- Develop greater problem-solving abilities
- Cope with the prior academic, job, or social failures
- Improve your self-esteem
- Learn how to strengthen connections with your family, co-workers, and friends
- Develop skills for regulating your temper

Common kinds of psychotherapy for ADHD include:

- Cognitive behavioral treatment. This systematic style of therapy provides particular strategies to regulate your behavior and turn negative thought patterns into good ones. It may help you manage life obstacles, such as school, job, or relationship problems, and help treat other mental health concerns, such as depression or drug addiction.

- Marital counseling and family therapy. This sort of treatment may assist loved ones deal with the stress of living with someone who has ADHD and understands what they can do to help. Such therapy helps enhance communication and problem-solving abilities.

Working on relationships

If you're like many people with ADHD, you may be unpredictable and forget appointments, skip deadlines and make hasty or illogical choices. These habits may tax the patience of the most forgiving co-worker, friend, or lover.

Therapy that focuses on these concerns and techniques to properly manage your behavior may be extremely useful. So can courses promote communication and build conflict resolution and problem-solving skills? Couples counseling and programs in which family members learn more about ADHD may dramatically enhance your relationships.

The necessity of receiving a professional examination for ADHD.

Seeking a professional diagnosis of Attention Deficit Hyperactivity Disorder (ADHD) is of the highest significance for numerous key reasons. While self-assessment or online quizzes may give first clues, a full examination done by a skilled healthcare professional or psychologist is needed for an accurate diagnosis and proper treatment. Here's why obtaining a professional examination for ADHD matters:

Accurate Diagnosis: ADHD is a complicated neurodevelopmental condition with a variety of symptoms and subtypes. Many other illnesses might appear with identical symptoms, such as anxiety, sadness, or learning impairments. A professional examination ensures that any possible underlying diseases are correctly recognized, leading to a more accurate diagnosis.

Differentiating from Normal Behavior: Some degree of inattention, impulsivity, or hyperactivity is usual in many persons, especially in specific settings. A professional examination helps differentiate between normal behavior and ADHD symptoms that adversely influence everyday living and functioning.

Early Intervention: If ADHD is present, early diagnosis and intervention may make a major impact on an individual's life. Early therapy may assist improve academic and vocational performance, promote self-esteem, and address any co-existing disorders or learning challenges.

Tailored Treatment Plan: Every individual with ADHD is unique, and a professional examination permits the formulation of a specific treatment plan. Depending on the degree of symptoms and the individual's unique circumstances, the treatment method may involve behavioral therapy, medication, or a mix of both.

Ruling Out Other variables: ADHD symptoms may be impacted by several variables, including stress, trauma, sleep difficulties, or medical issues. A full assessment helps rule out any underlying medical or psychological disorders contributing to the reported symptoms.

Medication Management: If medication is judged acceptable as part of the treatment plan, a professional assessment guarantees that the prescribed medicine is the most suited and safe alternative for the person. Regular monitoring and modifications may be conducted under expert direction.

Validation and Understanding: Receiving a formal diagnosis may give validation and understanding to people and their families. It helps explain the obstacles people confront and creates options for assistance and adjustments in academic, employment, or social situations.

Educational and Workplace suit: An official diagnosis of ADHD enables people to seek academic accommodations, such as additional time on examinations, or workplace accommodations, such as flexible scheduling, to suit their unique requirements.

Awareness and Coping Strategies: A professional examination may assist people and their families obtain a better understanding of ADHD and its effect. This information helps individuals to develop appropriate coping techniques and behavioral therapies to control symptoms more successfully.

Monitoring development: Regular assessments and follow-ups with healthcare specialists are required to monitor the individual's development, evaluate therapy effectiveness, and make any necessary revisions to the treatment plan.

Seeking a professional diagnosis for ADHD is a vital step toward understanding and treating the illness properly. It provides accurate diagnosis, tailored treatment planning, and access to relevant assistance and accommodations. Early intervention and thorough treatment may dramatically enhance the quality of life for those with ADHD, helping them excel academically, professionally, and emotionally.

The diagnostic criteria and evaluation method for adult ADHD.

The diagnostic criteria and evaluation method for adult ADHD follow principles established in the Diagnostic and Statistical Manual of Mental Disorders, Fifth Edition (DSM-5), published by the American Psychiatric Association. The procedure comprises a full examination undertaken by a competent healthcare expert, such as a psychiatrist, psychologist, or licensed mental health physician. Here is an outline of the diagnostic criteria and evaluation method for adult ADHD:

Symptom Presentation: The first stage in the evaluation procedure entails recognizing the presence of ADHD symptoms in adults. These symptoms are classified into two primary categories: inattention and hyperactivity/impulsivity.

- Inattention symptoms may include trouble maintaining attention, making thoughtless errors, difficulty organizing activities, forgetfulness, and being easily distracted.

- Hyperactivity/impulsivity symptoms may include restlessness, trouble keeping sitting, interrupting others, and impulsive decision-making.

Chronicity and Persistence: The healthcare expert will analyze if the individual's ADHD symptoms have been present from childhood and have lasted into adulthood. It is vital to confirm that the symptoms are not attributable to a recent or transient ailment.

Functional Impairment: The presence of ADHD symptoms alone is not sufficient for a diagnosis. The doctor must also prove that the symptoms severely affect the individual's social, intellectual, occupational, or personal functioning.

Rule Out any problems: The evaluation procedure entails ruling out any medical, psychological, or psychiatric problems that may be contributing to the reported symptoms. This procedure verifies that the symptoms are unique to ADHD and not caused by other reasons.

Full History: The healthcare practitioner will obtain a full developmental and medical history. They will question the individual's upbringing, academic achievement, behavioral habits, and family history to establish a lifetime pattern of ADHD symptoms.

Interviews and Questionnaires: The physician may undertake organized interviews with the individual and, if feasible, with family members or close friends to acquire a wider perspective on the person's behavior and symptoms. Standardized questionnaires or rating scales may also be used to measure ADHD symptoms and their effect.

Behavioral Observations: Observing the individual's behavior in different situations, such as work, home, or social surroundings, may give further insights regarding the existence and effect of ADHD symptoms.

Rule Out comorbid illnesses: Individuals with ADHD may also have comorbid illnesses, such as anxiety, depression, or learning difficulties. The evaluation method involves screening for the existence of any comorbidities to ensure complete treatment planning.

Educational or job background: Understanding the individual's educational or job background might give extra context about academic or vocational obstacles associated with ADHD symptoms.

Documentation: The healthcare professional will record the results and determine whether the person satisfies the particular criteria for an ADHD diagnosis based on the DSM-5 standards.

It is vital to note that diagnosing adult ADHD is a difficult procedure that involves clinical skill and a comprehensive assessment. The evaluation approach tries to diagnose ADHD precisely, rule out other possible causes of symptoms, and establish a thorough treatment plan customized to the individual's requirements. If an ADHD diagnosis is established, suitable therapies, such as behavioral therapy, medication, and lifestyle improvements, may dramatically enhance the individual's quality of life and help them better manage their symptoms.

Co-existing illnesses and their influence on ADHD treatment.

Recognizing co-existing disorders, often known as comorbidities, is a critical element of treating ADHD efficiently. Many persons with ADHD may have one or more other disorders that might impact their symptoms, treatment, and general well-being. Identifying and resolving these coexisting illnesses is critical for delivering comprehensive treatment and enhancing the overall management of ADHD. Here are some typical co-existing illnesses and their influence on ADHD management:

Anxiety problems: Anxiety problems commonly co-occur with ADHD. The presence of anxiety may worsen ADHD symptoms, leading to increased restlessness, trouble focusing, and impulsivity. Addressing anxiety via treatment and/or medication may assist improve ADHD management.

Depression: Depression is another prevalent comorbidity among persons with ADHD. It may intensify emotions of melancholy, pessimism, and poor energy, making it hard to manage ADHD-related issues. Treating depression with ADHD may enhance overall functioning and well-being.

Learning impairments: Some persons with ADHD may additionally have distinct learning impairments. These learning challenges may hinder academic achievement and produce dissatisfaction, hurting self-esteem and motivation. Identifying and resolving learning difficulties may lead to individualized educational interventions for improved academic achievement.

Substance Use Disorders: Adults with untreated ADHD may be at a greater risk of developing substance use disorders since they may resort to drugs or alcohol as a means to self-medicate or deal with their symptoms. Addressing both ADHD and drug use is critical for effective recovery.

Bipolar Disorder: Bipolar disorder may have characteristics with ADHD, such as impulsivity and mood swings. Distinguishing between the two illnesses is critical for optimal treatment planning and avoiding possible drug interactions.

Obsessive-obsessive Disorder (OCD): OCD may co-occur with ADHD, especially in situations where obsessive actions are utilized as a strategy to ease anxiety produced by ADHD symptoms. Treating OCD with ADHD may boost symptom control and overall performance.

Autism Spectrum Disorder (ASD): Some persons with ADHD may also have ASD. Diagnosing and managing both illnesses is crucial to guarantee targeted therapies that account for the particular requirements and problems associated with both disorders.

Sleep Disorders: Sleep issues are frequent in those with ADHD and may further influence attention, concentration, and impulsivity. Addressing sleep issues may enhance daytime functioning and ADHD symptom control.

Executive Functioning Deficits: Executive functioning deficits, such as difficulty with planning, organizing, and problem-solving, are typically evident in persons with ADHD. Addressing these impairments via focused therapies may boost everyday functioning.

Tic Disorders: Tic disorders, such as Tourette's syndrome, may occasionally coexist with ADHD. Managing tics and ADHD symptoms needs a holistic strategy that includes both diseases.

Understanding and managing comorbid illnesses are vital in building a complete treatment approach for patients with ADHD. A multidisciplinary strategy including healthcare practitioners from multiple specialties, such as psychiatry, psychology, and neurology, helps guarantee complete evaluation and therapy. Tailored therapies that target both ADHD and any accompanying diseases will lead to better results and improved overall quality of life for those with ADHD.

Impact on Daily Life

Living with attention-deficit hyperactivity disorder (ADHD) involves a broad series of issues that may make life more difficult and confusing. Those with ADHD may even ask, "Can a person with ADHD live a normal life?" Fortunately, once the condition is recognized, ADHD is easier to treat and manage than many other disorders. ADHD may also lead to enhanced creativity that may make you more effective in industries that need fresh techniques or ways of thinking.

Living with adult ADHD may make it difficult to concentrate on conversations or work. Some others may regard the activities of someone with ADHD as being scatterbrained, untidy, or sluggish. This stigma may make it more difficult for persons with ADHD to form connections and operate in a work setting.

What Does ADHD Feel Like?

ADHD feels like your mind and body are continually busy and that it is impossible to stop and concentrate. People with ADHD may feel like they would want to be able to switch off their thoughts for a few minutes or that they want to stop and relax, but simply can't. ADHD will be slightly different for each individual who has it. However, several symptoms are regularly reported.

How ADHD impacts work, relationships, and personal duties.

ADHD, or Attention Deficit Hyperactivity Disorder, may have a substantial influence on several parts of an individual's life, including employment, relationships, and personal duties. The symptoms of ADHD, such as inattention, hyperactivity, and impulsivity, may present issues in these areas, impairing everyday functioning and overall well-being. Here's how ADHD may affect employment, relationships, and personal responsibilities:

Work:

- Difficulty Sustaining concentration: Individuals with ADHD may find it tough to retain concentration on activities, resulting in lower productivity and frequent task-switching. This might result in incomplete work and issues reaching deadlines.
- Time Management Issues: Poor time management abilities are typical in ADHD. Individuals may fail to prioritize activities, estimate time effectively, and organize their work efficiently, resulting in missed deadlines and increased stress.
- Organization Challenges: ADHD may damage organizational abilities, making it tough to maintain workplaces neat and handle papers and supplies efficiently.
- Procrastination: Individuals with ADHD may struggle with commencing work and may procrastinate owing to

challenges in getting started or remaining motivated.

- Impulsivity at Work: Impulsive judgments and behaviors in the workplace may lead to blunders, misunderstandings, and disputes with coworkers or superiors.
- Job-Hopping: Adults with ADHD may suffer restlessness and discontent in particular work contexts, leading to repeated job changes.

Relationships:
- Inattention to Communication: Individuals with ADHD may have difficulties paying attention during talks, leading to misunderstandings and communication breakdowns in relationships.
- Forgetfulness: Forgetting crucial dates, obligations, or pledges may lead to dissatisfaction and disappointment among family members, friends, or partners.

- Impulsivity in Interactions: Impulsivity may lead to impetuous statements or acts that may inadvertently harm or offend others.
- Time Management in Relationships: Difficulties with time management might result in being repeatedly late for social engagements or appointments, harming relationships with others.
- Emotional Regulation: Emotional dysregulation is widespread in those with ADHD, impairing the capacity to manage arguments or disagreements calmly and sensibly.

Personal Responsibilities:
- Household Organization: Managing household duties, bills, and obligations may be problematic owing to issues in organization and time management.
- Financial Management: Impulsivity may lead to impulsive spending and

financial troubles, hurting the capacity to budget properly.

- Self-Care: Poor time management and forgetfulness may impair self-care habits, such as exercise, diet, and medication adherence.
- Academic Pursuits: Students with ADHD may have trouble with studying, managing schoolwork, and completing academic deadlines.
- Parenting Challenges: Adults with ADHD who are parents may find it tough to establish regular routines and respond to their children's needs consistently.

It is vital to remember that although ADHD may bring substantial obstacles, people with ADHD also possess distinct qualities and abilities. With proper therapies, support, and understanding, people may learn to manage their symptoms successfully and capitalize on their abilities. Behavioral therapy, medication, and lifestyle improvements are some of the tactics that may help persons with ADHD handle work, relationships, and personal obligations more effectively.

Building a supporting network of family, friends, and coworkers who understand ADHD and give encouragement is also helpful in conquering these issues. By adopting good coping tactics, time management strategies, and communication skills, persons with ADHD may lead full and successful lives in both personal and professional spheres.
Specific locations where ADHD-related problems are most obvious.

ADHD-related issues may emerge in numerous aspects of an individual's life. While the particular issues may differ from person to person, there are several general areas where ADHD-related obstacles are most obvious. These include:

Time Management: Individuals with ADHD generally suffer from time management, making it tough to organize, prioritize, and finish things in a timely way. They may have trouble predicting the time required for tasks, resulting in frequent lateness or missed deadlines.

Organization: ADHD may impact organizational abilities, making it tough to keep living spaces, work locations, or personal things neat and well-maintained. Individuals may have problems with organizing paperwork, timetables, or daily routines.

Attention and Focus: Inattention is a defining symptom of ADHD, leading to problems keeping focused on tasks, conversations, or academic or work-related activities. Individuals may get easily distracted and find it tough to focus for lengthy durations.

Impulsivity: Impulsive conduct is widespread in ADHD, prompting people to act without thinking about the implications. This impulsivity may impair decision-making, leading to hurried decisions and subsequent regrets.

Memory and Forgetfulness: Forgetfulness is a regular difficulty for those with ADHD. They may fail to recall meetings, obligations, or significant dates, leading to missed activities and increased stress.

Academic Performance: Students with ADHD may have issues in academic settings owing to difficulties with attention, time management, and organization. They may suffer uneven performance and difficulty with finishing projects and studying properly.

Job Performance: ADHD-related issues may impair job performance, leading to difficulty in keeping concentration, completing deadlines, and organizing duties. This may influence productivity and work happiness.

Emotional Regulation: Emotional dysregulation is frequent in persons with ADHD, leading to mood swings, heightened emotional reactions, and trouble dealing with irritation or stress.

Relationships: ADHD-related issues may impair personal relationships, notably in the areas of communication, forgetfulness, and time management. Difficulties with attention and impulsivity may lead to misunderstandings and disputes with family members, friends, or partners.

Driving and Safety: Hyperactivity and impulsivity may impair driving behavior and safety. Individuals with ADHD may be more prone to unsafe driving or accidents.

Financial Management: Impulsive spending and difficulty in planning and budgeting may lead to financial concerns for those with ADHD.

Self-Care: Poor time management and forgetfulness may impair self-care habits, such as exercise, diet, and medication adherence.

Identifying these particular areas of difficulty is critical for establishing focused therapies and support systems to assist persons with ADHD navigate their everyday lives more efficiently. A combination of behavioral treatment, medication, and lifestyle improvements may greatly improve ADHD management and promote overall functioning and well-being. Additionally, creating a supporting network of family, friends, and coworkers who understand ADHD and give encouragement may play a key role in helping those with ADHD flourish in all parts of their life.

CHAPTER 2

Coping Strategies and Techniques

Coping skills are crucial tools that people employ to manage both good and bad events in their everyday lives. These abilities aid in controlling stress and may have a substantial influence on physical and psychological well-being, eventually impacting one's capacity to perform at their best.

When it comes to mental health coping abilities, there are two primary types: problem-centered coping and emotion-centered coping. Understanding the contrast between these techniques may help people identify the most effective coping strategy for their personal requirements.

Problem-centered coping is useful when the emphasis is on improving the external circumstance. For instance, if someone is in an unhappy relationship, eliminating that source of stress from their life may drastically improve their overall stress levels. Problem-centered coping techniques handle external elements that contribute to mental health difficulties, such as personal connections and environmental pressures.

On the other side, emotion-centered coping mechanisms come into play when people are confronted with events they cannot control, such as the death of a loved one. In these situations, the objective is to care for one's emotional well-being and discover strategies to handle the emotional effect of the scenario. For persons suffering from chronic stress caused by mental health concerns, emotion-centered coping skills play a significant part in maintaining their everyday well-being.

By applying a mix of problem-centered and emotion-centered coping techniques, people may create a full toolset for effectively managing stress and preserving their mental health. Recognizing the value of these coping methods may empower people to proactively handle obstacles, build resilience, and promote overall emotional well-being.

Cognitive Behavioral Therapy (CBT)

CBT and its efficacy in controlling ADHD symptoms.

CBT, or Cognitive Behavioral Therapy, is a commonly used therapy strategy that focuses on recognizing and modifying negative thinking patterns and behaviors to enhance emotional regulation and general well-being. While CBT is not a cure for ADHD, it has been demonstrated to be useful in treating ADHD symptoms and improving functional results for those with the disease.

Here's how CBT works and its efficacy in reducing ADHD symptoms:
How CBT Works:

Identifying Thinking Patterns: CBT begins by helping clients become aware of their negative thinking patterns and cognitive distortions connected to their ADHD symptoms. These may include emotions of inadequacy, irritation, or self-doubt.

Changing Negative Ideas: With the guidance of a qualified therapist, people learn to confront and reframe these negative ideas. They create more balanced and sensible ways of processing circumstances, minimizing emotional discomfort and boosting coping skills.

Behavioral Strategies: CBT also contains behavioral treatments. Individuals with ADHD are given practical skills, such as time management tactics, organizing strategies, and goal-setting, to increase their everyday functioning.

Problem-Solving Skills: CBT prepares persons with ADHD with problem-solving skills to tackle obstacles that may occur owing to their symptoms. They learn to identify viable solutions and assess their efficacy.

Emotion Regulation: CBT focuses on helping people regulate their emotions properly. They learn coping methods to manage frustration, impatience, and stress in healthy ways.

Effectiveness in Managing ADHD Symptoms:

Improved Time Management: CBT helps persons with ADHD develop better time management skills, making it simpler to organize and prioritize work successfully.

Enhanced Focus and Attention: By learning to combat distractibility and enhance attention, people may remain more involved and focused on projects.

Organization and Planning: CBT offers persons with ADHD organizational skills and planning strategies to handle their duties more effectively.

Reduced Impulsivity: CBT tackles impulsivity by helping people learn methods to stop and consider before acting, leading to improved decision-making.

Improved Academic and Work Performance: With the guidance of CBT, persons with ADHD may build good study or work routines, leading to greater performance and results.

Enhanced Emotional Regulation: CBT helps people to detect and control their emotions better, lowering emotional reactivity and enhancing emotional well-being.

Greater Self-Awareness: Through CBT, persons with ADHD gain insight into their strengths and weaknesses. This self-awareness may promote self-esteem and support personal progress.

Long-Term Benefits: The skills taught in CBT may have enduring impacts beyond treatment sessions, allowing patients to continue employing these approaches throughout their life.

It's crucial to remember that the efficacy of CBT in addressing ADHD symptoms might differ across people. Some may notice major benefits, while others may encounter more moderate alterations. For many persons with ADHD, a combination of CBT, medication, and other supportive therapies may be very useful in controlling symptoms and boosting overall functioning and well-being.

Negative thinking patterns and replacing them with good ones.

Identifying negative thinking patterns and replacing them with positive ones is a key part of cognitive behavioral therapy (CBT) and may be useful for those looking to enhance their emotional well-being and coping abilities. Here's step-by-step guidance on how to detect and replace negative thinking patterns with positive ones:

Self-Awareness:

- Pay attention to your thoughts: Start by being aware of your thoughts and how they affect your emotions and behavior. Notice patterns of negative thinking, such as self-criticism, catastrophizing, or overgeneralization.

Challenge Negative Thoughts:

- Question the evidence: When you notice yourself thinking a negative idea, ask yourself if there is solid evidence to back it. Often, negative sentiments are founded on assumptions or misunderstandings.
- Consider alternate explanations: Explore alternative viewpoints or explanations for the issue. This might help you perceive things from a more balanced and realistic perspective.

Cognitive Restructuring:

- Replace negative thinking: Once you've questioned bad notions, replace them with more optimistic and realistic ones. Use affirmations, positive self-talk, or evidence-based assertions to overcome negative beliefs.

Practice Positive Affirmations:

- Create positive statements: Develop a list of positive affirmations that correspond with your aims and beliefs. Repeat these affirmations consistently to promote good thought habits.

Gratitude Practice:

- Focus on gratitude: Cultivate a practice of concentrating on things you are thankful for each day. This might help alter your mentality from obsessing about issues to enjoying the positives.

Mindfulness Meditation:

- Practice mindfulness: Engage in mindfulness meditation or activities to become more aware of your thoughts without judgment. Mindfulness may help you recognize unpleasant ideas without getting caught up in them.

Journaling:

- Write in a diary: Keep a journal to record your ideas and feelings frequently. Writing may help you process unpleasant emotions and provide insights into habits of thought.

Seek Support:

- Share with others: Talk to a trustworthy friend, family member, or therapist about your unpleasant thoughts and feelings. Sharing may bring perspective and emotional support.

Challenge Perfectionism:

- Embrace imperfection: Recognize that it's alright to make errors and not be flawless. Set reasonable expectations for yourself and applaud achievement, no matter how tiny.

Focus on Solutions:

- Problem-solving orientation: Shift your emphasis from brooding on issues to actively finding answers. Develop problem-solving abilities to face issues constructively.

Remember that changing negative thinking patterns with good ones requires work and patience. Be kind to yourself and give space for self-compassion. Over time, continuously adopting these tactics may lead to more positive thought patterns, increased emotional well-being, and enhanced coping abilities to negotiate life's problems more successfully. If you find it tough to manage negative ideas on your own, consider obtaining guidance from a mental health professional who can lead you through the process of cognitive restructuring and give you extra tools to support your path toward a more optimistic mentality.

Coping methods to cope with impulsivity and inattention.

Developing coping strategies to cope with impulsivity and inattention is critical for those with ADHD. These abilities may help manage symptoms efficiently, boost attention, and improve general daily functioning. Here are some coping tactics to overcome impulsivity and inattention:

Break Tasks into Smaller Steps:
- Divide major jobs or projects into smaller, doable segments. This technique makes chores less intimidating and helps you remain focused on finishing each stage before moving on to the next.

Use Timers and Alarms:
- Set timers or utilize alarms on your phone or a specialized device to remind you to start or complete work, meetings, or appointments. This method helps enhance time

management and prevent forgetfulness.

Create To-Do Lists:

- Develop daily to-do lists, prioritizing things based on urgency and significance. Crossing off finished activities creates a feeling of success and keeps you organized.

Utilize Visual Reminders:

- Place visual reminders, such as sticky notes or calendars, in prominent areas to assist recall key events, deadlines, or obligations.

Practice Mindfulness:

- Engage in mindfulness exercises to increase present-moment awareness and minimize impulsivity. Techniques such as deep breathing or grounding exercises might help recover concentration.

Delay Gratification:

- When confronted with impulsive choices, try postponing gratification. Take time to ponder the ramifications of your actions before making a decision.

Self-Reflection and Evaluation:

- Regularly reflect on impulsive judgments or inattentive acts. Identify trends and triggers to better understand your actions and work on improving them.

Implement Structured Routines:

- Establish established daily routines that include set hours for work, breaks, meals, and leisure activities. Routines may decrease impulsivity and boost attention.

Limit Distractions:

- Minimize environmental distractions when working or studying. Create a clutter-free workstation and switch off alerts on smart gadgets as required.

Practice Active Listening:
- Improve attention and listening abilities by actively participating in discussions. Avoid interrupting others and employ strategies

Time Management and Organization

Strategies for successful time management and prioritizing work.

Time management and organizing may be especially tough for individuals with Attention Deficit Hyperactivity Disorder (ADHD) owing to the difficulty in sustaining attention, prioritizing work, and keeping concentration. However, with the correct tools and accommodations, persons with ADHD may improve their time management and organizing abilities. Here are some special advice suited to adults with ADHD:

1. Use Visual Aids: Visual cues may be incredibly effective for those with ADHD. Utilize color-coded calendars, to-do lists, and sticky notes to reflect distinct projects and deadlines. Display the schedule

conspicuously in your workstation or living environment to keep on track.

2. Set Reminders and Alarms: Leverage technology to set reminders and alarms for appointments, deadlines, and critical activities. Smartphones and other technological gadgets may serve as essential tools to keep you on schedule.

3. Break jobs into Smaller Steps: Large jobs might seem daunting, leading to procrastination. Break them down into smaller, more doable stages. Celebrate the accomplishment of each stage to keep motivated.

4. Use Time Blocking: Allocate distinct blocks of time for various jobs and activities. Set distinct start and finish timings for each block to create an organized habit.

5. Limit Distractions: Minimize distractions in your area as much as possible. Create a

defined workstation that is free from clutter and noise.

6. Set Realistic Expectations: Be realistic about what you can do in a given length of time. Avoid filling your calendar with too many tasks, since this may lead to dissatisfaction and disappointment.

7. Incorporate Regular pauses: Adults with ADHD may benefit from including regular pauses throughout work. Use tactics like the Pomodoro Technique (working in short periods with pauses) to retain attention and minimize burnout.

8. Externalize Memory: Use external tools like planners, digital calendars, or task management applications to unload the strain of remembering everything in your mind.

9. Seek Accountability and Support: Share your objectives and plans with a trusted

friend, family member, or coach who can give accountability and support.

10. Practice Mindfulness: Mindfulness practices, such as meditation or deep breathing exercises, may assist enhance concentration and attention. Regular practice may help relieve stress and promote self-awareness.

11. Consider Professional Support: Work with a therapist or coach who specializes in ADHD to build tailored methods and coping mechanisms.

12. Reward Yourself: Implement a reward system for finishing chores or keeping organized. good reinforcement may help promote good actions.

13. Be Kind to Yourself: Managing ADHD may be tough, and setbacks are common. Be patient and kind to yourself during the process.

14. Medication (if prescribed): Some individuals with ADHD find that medication may considerably enhance their ability to manage time and remain organized. If prescribed, work carefully with a healthcare practitioner to discover the proper drug and dose.

15. Develop Consistent Routines: Establishing consistent daily routines may help persons with ADHD transition between activities more effortlessly and decrease decision fatigue.

Remember that everyone's experience with ADHD is unique, so it may take time to discover the mix of tactics that works best for you. Be open to experimenting with new ways and seeking expert help if required. With patience, effort, and the correct help, individuals with ADHD may learn efficient time management and organizing skills to lead satisfying and successful lives.

Implement tools and approaches for improved organizing.

Implementing tools and practices for a better organization may considerably enhance your productivity, decrease stress, and help you keep on top of your activities and obligations. Here are some excellent tools and strategies to consider:

Digital Calendars: Use digital calendars like Google Calendar, Outlook, or Apple Calendar to plan appointments, deadlines, and activities. Set up reminders to get alerts before crucial occasions.

Task Management applications: Utilize task management applications like Todoist, Trello, or Asana to build to-do lists and monitor your tasks. These applications frequently let you set due dates, prioritize tasks, and classify them based on projects or areas of concentration.

Note-Taking applications: Keep track of ideas, critical information, and notes with applications like Evernote or Microsoft OneNote. These programs enable you to arrange notes into notebooks or categories for quick reference.

Time Blocking: Allocate distinct blocks of time for various jobs and activities. Use a timer to keep focused throughout each block, and take brief pauses between jobs.

Kanban Boards: Create a physical or digital Kanban board to see your tasks and progress. Use sticky notes or cards to represent tasks and move them through various phases (e.g., to-do, in progress, done).

Color-Coding: Apply color-coding to your calendars, folders, and notes to rapidly differentiate between various tasks, projects, or categories.

Checklists: Develop checklists for recurrent chores or routines. This might be particularly beneficial for daily or weekly activities and commitments.

Mind Mapping: Use mind maps to brainstorm ideas, organize tasks, and link similar thoughts graphically.

Email Management: Keep your email organized by establishing folders and using labels or tags to classify incoming messages. Set aside defined periods to check and reply to emails to prevent continual distractions.

Cloud Storage: Use cloud storage services like Google Drive, Dropbox, or Microsoft OneDrive to keep your information accessible across devices and well-organized.

Tidy Regularly: Regularly tidy your physical and digital environments to remove superfluous stuff and decrease distractions.

Physical Planners: If you prefer a practical method, try using a physical planner or bullet journal to manage your chores and calendar.

Automate Repetitive processes: Where feasible, automate repetitive processes using platforms like IFTTT or Zapier to save time and effort.

Use Reminders: Set reminders on your phone or wristwatch to urge you to perform specified chores or take medicine, if required.

Establish a Home for Everything: Designate particular areas for commonly used goods to avoid misplacement and save time hunting for them afterward.

Batch comparable jobs: Group comparable jobs together and handle them in one go. For instance, react to emails, make phone calls, or execute administrative activities consistently.

Weekly Reviews: Conduct weekly reviews to analyze progress, plan the next week, and make improvements to your organizing structure as appropriate.

Remember that finding the optimal mix of tools and strategies is a personal experience. Experiment with several ways to see what works best for you and supports your natural organizing style. Consistency and dedication in applying these tools and approaches can help you maintain superior organization in both your personal and professional life.

Create routines to minimize stress and boost productivity.

Creating routines may be an effective strategy to decrease stress, enhance productivity, and retain a feeling of consistency and control in your everyday life. Routines give structure and assist automate some chores, freeing up brain resources for more essential choices. Here's how you can construct powerful routines:

Identify Priorities: Determine the most crucial aspects of your life that might benefit from regularity, such as morning/evening routines, work/study routines, exercise, or self-care.

Start Small: Begin with only one or two routines and progressively increase as you grow more familiar with the process.

Morning Routine: Design a morning routine that sets a good tone for the day. This may involve things like getting up at a regular time, stretching or exercising, meditating, eating a good breakfast, and preparing your day.

Evening Routine: Create an evening routine to wind down and prepare for a pleasant night's sleep. Consider things like setting aside time for relaxation, avoiding electronics before night, and preparing your home for the following day.

Block Time for Certain Tasks: Schedule blocks of time throughout your day for certain tasks, such as work, studying, or creative endeavors. Try to establish a regular schedule to create a habit.

Set Reminders: Use alarms or alerts on your phone or computer to remind you of normal tasks. This might be especially beneficial when establishing a new regimen.

Be reasonable: Ensure your routines are reasonable and feasible. Avoid crowding your schedule, as it may lead to irritation and abandonment of the habit.

Flexibility is Key: While routines give structure, it's crucial to remain adaptable when unexpected circumstances emerge. Adapt your regimen as required, and don't be too harsh on yourself if you skip a step.

Incorporate pauses: Include brief pauses in your routines to minimize burnout and retain attention throughout work or study sessions.

Stay Mindful of Time: Keep track of time throughout your routine to avoid things from lasting longer than expected.

Account for Personal requirements: Tailor your routines to your particular requirements and preferences. What works for someone else may not work for you.

Reward Yourself: Include little prizes for completing routines or specialized activities to inspire yourself and reinforce good behavior.

Assess and Adjust: Regularly assess your routines to see what's working and what needs improvement. Adjust the routines as required to best fit your lifestyle.

Incorporate Self-Care: Include self-care activities in your routines, such as exercise, mindfulness, or spending time with loved ones.

Consistency is Key: Stick to your routines regularly to transform them into habits. It may take time and effort, but the more you follow the program, the simpler it gets.

Remember that routines should act as a tool to enhance your well-being and productivity, not as a cause of stress themselves. Experiment with various routines and techniques until you discover a balance that works for you. Over time, a well-crafted routine may become an integral part of your daily life, helping you minimize stress and accomplish your objectives more successfully.

Improving Focus and Attention

Techniques to enhance attention and concentration in everyday tasks.

Improving attention and concentration in everyday tasks may boost productivity and overall performance. Here are some strategies to help you remain focused and concentrate better:

Create a Distraction-Free Environment: Minimize distractions in your workstation or study location. Turn off alerts on your phone or utilize programs that block distracting websites during concentrated work hours.

Use Time Blocking: Set precise time blocks for jobs or activities. During these concentrated intervals, avoid multitasking and concentrate entirely on the subject at hand.

Practice the Pomodoro Technique: Work in short, concentrated intervals (e.g., 25 minutes) followed by a brief rest (e.g., 5 minutes). After completing multiple intervals, take a longer lengthier pause (e.g., 15-30 minutes).

Set Clear Objectives: Define clear and realistic objectives for each action. Knowing what you want to achieve helps retain concentration and direction.

Prioritize Tasks: Identify the most critical tasks and handle them first. This minimizes feeling overwhelmed and ensures vital activities get finished.

Break jobs into Smaller segments: Divide major jobs into smaller, more manageable segments. This makes it easy to remain focused and measure progress.

Practice Mindfulness: Engage in mindfulness techniques, such as meditation or deep breathing, to educate your mind to remain present and decrease distractions.

Eliminate Mental Clutter: Jot down distracting ideas or chores on a notepad to free mental space and return to them later.

Stay Organized: Use tools like calendars, to-do lists, and digital applications to keep track of projects, deadlines, and appointments.

Take Regular pauses: Give yourself regular pauses throughout the day to rejuvenate and avoid mental tiredness.

Stay Hydrated and Eat Nutritious Meals: Proper hydration and a balanced diet may significantly improve attention and cognitive performance.

Exercise Regularly: Physical exercise may enhance blood flow to the brain and assist maintain mental alertness.

Practice Deep Work: Allocate longer periods of uninterrupted time for more demanding activities that need deep attention.

Use Visualization Techniques: Picture yourself successfully completing a job or project, improving motivation and attention.

Use Focus Aids: Consider utilizing tools like noise-canceling headphones, background music, or white noise to create a concentrated work atmosphere.

Chunk material: When studying or learning, split the material into smaller chunks and review one at a time.

Receive Sufficient Sleep: Ensure you receive enough restful sleep each night to revitalize your mind for improved concentration throughout the day.

Limit Stimulants: Reduce or eliminate excessive coffee and other stimulants that may disturb attention and concentration.

Practice Active Listening: Stay involved throughout talks or meetings by actively listening and asking questions for greater recall.

Reward Yourself: Set up a reward system to recognize victories and sustain motivation.

Remember that increasing attention and concentration is a skill that needs practice and patience. Experiment with these strategies and determine what works best for you. Be persistent in adopting them, and with time, you'll see gains in your ability to remain focused and concentrate efficiently on everyday tasks.

Mindfulness and meditation methods for adults with ADHD.

Mindfulness and meditation activities may be especially effective for individuals with ADHD since they can assist increase attention, decrease impulsivity, and boost self-awareness. Here are some mindfulness and meditation methods geared toward those with ADHD:

Breathing techniques: Practice deep breathing techniques to soothe the mind and body. Focus on your breath and examine its rhythm and feeling.

Body Scan: Perform a body scan meditation by paying attention to each area of your body, from head to toe, observing any tension or discomfort.

Guided Meditation: Use guided meditation sessions particularly developed for ADHD.

These sessions frequently give instructions and visuals to assist keep the mind focused.

Mindful Walking: Engage in mindful walking by concentrating on the feeling of each step, the movement of your body, and the surroundings around you.

Five Senses Exercise: Take a minute to observe and explain five things you can see, four things you can touch, three things you can hear, two things you can smell, and one item you can taste. This technique might help anchor you in the present moment.

Mindful Eating: Eat consciously, paying attention to the flavor, texture, and experience of each mouthful. Avoid distractions when eating, such as watching TV or using your phone.

S.T.O.P. Technique: When you feel overwhelmed or distracted, apply the S.T.O.P. technique: Stop, Take a breath,

Observe your thoughts and emotions, and Proceed carefully.

Loving-compassion Meditation: Practice spreading love and compassion to yourself and others. This may promote self-compassion and empathy.

Focus on One Activity at a Time: Use mindfulness to focus on one activity at a time, giving it your entire attention before moving on to the next.

Acceptance and Non-Judgment: Practice accepting your ideas and emotions without judgment. Let's get rid of self-criticism and adopt a non-judgmental mindset.

Meditation applications: Utilize meditation applications like Headspace, Calm, or Insight Timer, which provide guided meditations and mindfulness activities.

Meditation Groups or Courses: Join meditation groups or courses in your town or online. Group settings may give support and encouragement for frequent practice.

Mindful Listening: When in discussion, devote your complete attention to the speaker. Practice active listening without interrupting or forming replies in your head.

Regular Practice: Establish a constant meditation regimen, even if it's only a few minutes each day. Regular practice may lead to more substantial advantages over time.

Be Patient and Gentle: Be patient with yourself throughout meditation and mindfulness practice. Acknowledge that your mind may wander, and gently bring your concentration back to the present moment.

Mindfulness and meditation are abilities that take constant practice to acquire. It's crucial to approach these disciplines with an open mind and a desire to explore alternative ways. Over time, you may see gains in your ability to concentrate, regulate impulses, and develop better self-awareness as an adult with ADHD.

Set reasonable objectives and divide work into small stages.

Setting realistic objectives and dividing work into manageable chunks are key tactics for enhancing productivity and attaining success. Here's how to successfully utilize these techniques:

1. Define Clear and precise objectives: Start by creating clear, precise, and realistic objectives. Ensure that your goals are well-defined and have a particular consequence.

2. Prioritize Your Objectives: Identify the most critical objectives and rank them based on their relevance and urgency. Focus on a few major objectives at a time to prevent getting overwhelmed.

3. Break Down Goals into Smaller Activities: Divide each large goal into smaller, practical activities. This makes things less overwhelming and more doable.

4. Use the SMART Goal Framework: Ensure your objectives are Specific, Measurable, Achievable, Relevant, and Time-bound. This framework helps you define reasonable and achievable goals.

5. Set Realistic Timeframes: Allocate realistic timeframes for finishing each activity. Avoid establishing unreasonable timelines that could lead to disappointment or hasten the process.

6. Create Task Lists: Make thorough to-do lists for each objective, including all the actions necessary to fulfill it. Check off completed activities to measure progress and remain motivated.

7. attention on One Task at a Time: Avoid multitasking, since it may impair productivity and attention. Concentrate on one activity at a time, and once accomplished, go on to the next.

8. Use Time Blocking: Allocate specified time blocks for each job on your to-do list. Stick to these time restrictions to ensure you're committing enough time to accomplish each stage.

9. Be Flexible and Adaptive: Be open to altering your objectives and strategies as required. Life is unpredictable, and sometimes you need to modify your strategy to attain success.

10. Celebrate Milestones: Acknowledge and celebrate your progress when you accomplish each task or achieve milestones. Positive reinforcement may enhance motivation and morale.

11. seek assistance and assign: If some activities demand skills or experience outside your scope, don't hesitate to seek assistance or assign them to others.

12. examine and Adjust: Regularly examine your progress and revisit your objectives and assignments. Adjust your plans if required, and learn from any failures.

13. Focus on Process Over Outcome: Concentrate on the work and progress you're making rather than just fixating on the ultimate result. Acknowledge the steps you're taking toward your objectives.

14. Practice Self-Compassion: Be compassionate to yourself if you endure

hardships or disappointments. Don't be too harsh on yourself and realize that development takes time.

15. Seek Accountability: Share your objectives with a friend, mentor, or coach who can keep you responsible and give support along the way.

By defining realistic goals and dividing activities into manageable chunks, you may make substantial progress toward reaching your objectives. This strategy lowers feelings of overload, promotes concentration, and enables you to remain on track, eventually leading to better achievement and a sense of accomplishment.

CHAPTER 3

Medication and Lifestyle Adjustments

The advantages and probable adverse effects of medicine.

Medications may be a beneficial therapy choice for different physical illnesses, including mental health issues. It's crucial to understand both the advantages and possible adverse effects of drugs before commencing any therapy. Here's everything you need to know:

Benefits of Medication:
Symptom Management: Medications may successfully treat and reduce symptoms of medical illnesses, such as depression, anxiety, ADHD, and more.

Improved Quality of Life: By lowering symptoms, drugs may enhance the overall quality of life, helping persons function better in their everyday activities.

Enhanced performance: For certain disorders, medicines may assist enhance cognitive performance, attention, concentration, and memory.

Stabilization: Medications may give stability to persons with illnesses like bipolar disorder, minimizing excessive mood swings.

Prevention of Complications: In certain circumstances, drugs may prevent complications and advancement of certain medical disorders.

Treatment of Physical Issues: Medications are commonly used to control physical health issues, such as infections, persistent pain, or heart disease.

Support in Therapy: Medications may complement and support the efficacy of therapy and other non-pharmacological therapies.

Potential Side Effects:

Common adverse Effects: Some drugs may produce minor and short-term adverse effects, such as drowsiness, dizziness, nausea, or dry mouth. These adverse effects frequently subside over time.

Major Side Effects: In rare situations, drugs may lead to major side effects that need rapid medical treatment, such as allergic responses or severe mood changes.

Drug Interactions: treatments may interact with other drugs or substances, leading to undesirable effects or lowering the efficacy of one or both treatments.

Tolerance and Dependency: Some drugs may develop tolerance, where the original dosage becomes less effective over time. Additionally, certain drugs might produce dependence or withdrawal symptoms if withdrawn suddenly.

Weight Gain or Loss: Certain drugs may be connected with weight gain or loss, which may impair certain persons' self-esteem and general well-being.

Sexual Dysfunction: Some drugs may contribute to sexual adverse effects, such as reduced libido or difficulties attaining or sustaining erections.

Liver and Kidney Function: Certain drugs may impact liver or kidney function, necessitating frequent monitoring via blood testing.

Pregnancy and nursing hazards: It's crucial to recognize the possible hazards of taking drugs during pregnancy or while nursing.

It's vital to have an open and honest talk with your healthcare professional before taking any medicine. They may analyze your medical history, explain possible advantages and side effects, and help you make an educated choice about the best-suited treatment method for your unique situation. Additionally, frequent follow-up consultations with your healthcare practitioner are crucial to evaluate your reaction to the medicine and address any concerns or side effects that may occur.

Work closely with a healthcare expert for medication management.

Working closely with a healthcare expert for drug management is of vital significance for various reasons. Whether you're beginning a new medicine or changing an old one, having the counsel and support of a trained healthcare practitioner is crucial. Here are some reasons why it's vital to consult with a healthcare expert for drug management:

Accurate Diagnosis: A healthcare expert can properly diagnose your medical issue and decide whether medication is a suitable treatment choice. They will assess your symptoms, medical history, and any other relevant circumstances.

Customized Treatment Plan: Healthcare experts build customized treatment programs according to your unique requirements and medical history. They analyze criteria including age, sex, other health issues, and potential medication interactions to guarantee the best possible result.

Choosing the Right Medication: There are typically many drugs available for treating the same illness. A healthcare practitioner will assist you pick the most suited drug based on its efficacy, side effect profile, and unique circumstances.

Dose and Timing: Healthcare experts will prescribe the right dose and offer advice on when and how to take the drug. This ensures that you are taking the proper quantity of medicine at the relevant times.

Monitoring and Adjustment: Regular follow-up sessions enable healthcare providers to check your reaction to the drug. They may make modifications to the dose or switch to a different drug if required to enhance treatment results.

Managing Side Effects: Healthcare practitioners may treat any side effects or unpleasant reactions that may develop during pharmaceutical usage. They can assist control these consequences and identify other options when required.

Avoiding Drug Interactions: Healthcare experts are educated about possible drug interactions that might arise while taking various drugs concurrently. They will examine any possible dangers and modify prescriptions appropriately.

Pharmaceutical Safety: Healthcare workers remain up-to-date on the latest research, safety recommendations, and best practices related to pharmaceutical usage. They may tell you of any safety risks linked to the medicine.

Education and Information: A healthcare practitioner will offer you vital information regarding the medicine, including how it works, possible advantages, and what to anticipate throughout treatment.

Long-Term Management: For chronic illnesses, continual medication management is important. Regular meetings with a healthcare expert ensure that your treatment plan stays successful over time.

Advocacy and Support: Your healthcare professional may be your advocate, helping you through the complexity of the healthcare system and advocating for your best interests.

Empowerment and Informed Decision-Making: Working closely with a healthcare provider helps you to actively engage in your treatment choices. You may ask questions, express concerns, and make educated decisions about your health.

Remember that open communication with your healthcare practitioner is vital. Be honest about your symptoms, experiences, and any worries you may have. Working together as a team ensures that you get the best possible treatment and optimize the advantages of medicine while limiting any hazards.

Healthy Lifestyle Habits

The importance of exercise, diet, and sleep in controlling ADHD symptoms.

Exercise, diet, and sleep play key roles in controlling ADHD (Attention Deficit Hyperactivity Disorder) symptoms and may have a good influence on general well-being. Here's how each of these elements helps to treat ADHD symptoms:

1. Exercise:
Physical activity, such as aerobic workouts, may assist enhance attention, concentration, and cognitive function in persons with ADHD.
Exercise promotes the release of neurotransmitters like dopamine and norepinephrine, which are critical for controlling attention and mood.
Regular exercise helps lower hyperactivity and impulsivity, producing a calmer state of mind.

Participating in sports or other physical activities may also give a healthy outlet for surplus energy, decreasing restlessness and fidgeting.

2. Nutrition:
A healthy diet rich in key nutrients may favorably affect brain function and help control ADHD symptoms.
Omega-3 fatty acids, found in fish, nuts, and seeds, have shown potential advantages in lowering inattention and hyperactivity in certain persons with ADHD.
Protein-rich diets may help regulate blood sugar levels, minimizing swings in energy and attention.
Avoiding excessive sugar and highly processed meals may assist maintain steady energy levels and minimize mood swings.

3. Sleep:
Sufficient and restful sleep is necessary for good brain function and emotional stability.

Lack of sleep may aggravate ADHD symptoms, leading to increased impulsivity, inattention, and irritability.

Establishing regular sleep patterns and keeping a relaxing sleep environment may enhance sleep quality in persons with ADHD.

4. Managing Stress:

Chronic stress may increase ADHD symptoms, making it vital to manage stress with relaxation strategies, such as mindfulness, meditation, or deep breathing exercises.

Engaging in hobbies or activities that offer pleasure and relaxation may also help lower stress levels.

It's crucial to remember that although exercise, diet, and sleep might be good for controlling ADHD symptoms, they are not single remedies. They perform best when used in tandem with other evidence-based therapies, such as behavioral therapy or medication (if recommended). Each individual with ADHD is unique, and what works well for one person may vary for another.

Consulting with healthcare specialists, including physicians, psychologists, or registered dietitians, may give tailored assistance on how to incorporate exercise, nutrition, and sleep into a holistic ADHD treatment strategy. Additionally, integrating family members and instructors in the management process helps provide a supportive atmosphere for those with ADHD to flourish.

Strategies for lowering stress and regulating emotional well-being.

Reducing stress and controlling emotional well-being is vital for sustaining overall health and dealing with life's obstacles efficiently. Here are some techniques to assist you establish a better balance and enhance your emotional well-being:

Practice Mindfulness and Meditation: Engage in mindfulness exercises and meditation to remain present, decrease anxiety, and build emotional resilience.

Exercise Regularly: Physical exercise may produce endorphins, which are natural mood boosters. Regular exercise may help relieve stress and promote mental well-being.

Maintain a Balanced Diet: Eat healthy meals, including fruits, vegetables, whole grains, and lean meats, to support your body and mind.

Get Adequate Sleep: Prioritize quality sleep since it is vital for emotional control and general well-being.

Set Realistic objectives: Set feasible and manageable objectives to prevent feeling overwhelmed and harassed by unrealistic expectations.

Learn to Say No: Establish healthy boundaries and learn to say no to obligations that may overload you or threaten your well-being.

Connect with Supportive People: Spend time with friends, family, or support groups to establish meaningful ties and social support.

Engage in Relaxation methods: Incorporate relaxation methods such as deep breathing, progressive muscle relaxation, or yoga to decrease tension and increase peace.

Limit Exposure to Stressors: Identify and reduce exposure to stressors in your surroundings, where feasible. This may involve creating boundaries with negative influencers or restricting exposure to disturbing news or media.

Seek Professional Help: If stress becomes unbearable, consider obtaining help from a therapist or counselor to deal with emotional difficulties.

Practice Self-Compassion: Be gentle to yourself and avoid self-criticism. Treat yourself with the same kindness you would give a friend experiencing comparable circumstances.

Engage in Hobbies: Participate in things you like and that provide you a feeling of satisfaction and pleasure.

Express feelings: Find healthy methods to express feelings, such as via writing, painting, or chatting with a supportive friend.

Limit Caffeine and Alcohol: Excessive caffeine and alcohol use might add to emotions of worry and tension. Moderation is crucial.

Create a Supportive Environment: Surround yourself with good influences, inspirational settings, and things that bring you delight.

Limit Screen Time: Reduce screen time on electronics and social media, since excessive exposure may lead to stress and emotional overload.

Practice thankfulness: Cultivate thankfulness by consistently noticing and appreciating the wonderful parts of your life.

Volunteer or Help Others: Giving back and helping others may build a feeling of purpose and contribute to mental well-being.

Remember that managing stress and emotional well-being is a continuous process that may involve experimentation to determine what works best for you. Implementing a mix of these tactics may provide a basis for a better, more balanced, and more rewarding existence. If you encounter ongoing emotional issues or stress, consider getting help from a mental health professional for individualized support and coping skills.

Limit distractions and establish an ADHD-friendly atmosphere.

Limiting distractions and developing an ADHD-friendly atmosphere may greatly enhance attention and productivity for those with Attention Deficit Hyperactivity Disorder (ADHD). Here are various techniques to do this:

Organize Your Space: Keep your workstation, home, and study environments clean, clutter-free, and well-organized. A clean setting may eliminate visual distractions and help you remain focused.

Designate a Specific Workspace: Create a defined location for work or study where you may link the environment with focus and productivity.

Minimize Noise: Reduce auditory distractions by wearing noise-canceling headphones or playing relaxing background music, instrumental music, or white noise.

Limit Visual Distractions: Close unneeded tabs or windows on your computer, put away non-essential stuff, and utilize desk organizers to make vital information conveniently accessible.

Set Boundaries with Others: Communicate with family members, roommates, or coworkers about your need for a distraction-free atmosphere during particular times.

Time Block for Focus: Allocate dedicated time blocks for concentrated work or study. Inform people about your concentrated time to prevent disruptions.

Use Time Management Strategies: Implement time management strategies like the Pomodoro Technique (working in short periods with breaks) to retain concentration.

Prioritize Tasks: Identify the most essential tasks for the day and concentrate on finishing them first before moving on to less crucial activities.

Turn Off Notifications: Silence or turn off notifications on your phone, computer, or other electronic devices during concentrated work hours.

Use Focus Aids: Utilize applications or browser plugins that block distracting websites or place limitations on your internet usage.

Color-Coding: Use color-coding to organize jobs or resources, making it simpler to locate what you need without being sidetracked.

Break jobs into Smaller stages: Divide major jobs into smaller, more manageable stages to minimize feeling overwhelmed.

Keep a To-Do List: Write down projects and deadlines on a to-do list to keep organized and focused.

Use Visual Timers: Set visual timers to assist you judge how much time you have left for a task, which may aid in remaining on track.

Limit Access to Temptations: If some products or activities are very distracting, try eliminating them from your desk during concentrated moments.

Practice Mindfulness: Engage in mindfulness activities to teach your mind to be present and concentrate when distractions emerge.

Seek cooperation from Others: Communicate your requirements to friends, family, or colleagues, and ask for their cooperation in building an ADHD-friendly atmosphere.

Remember that developing an ADHD-friendly atmosphere is a customized process. Experiment with various tactics to determine what works best for you and boosts your ability to focus and handle distractions successfully. Over time, with constant work, you may adjust your surroundings to promote your productivity and general well-being.

Build a Support Systems

The necessity of getting help from family, friends, and coworkers.

Seeking assistance from family, friends, and coworkers is of the highest significance for numerous parts of our life, including personal well-being, mental health, and professional progress. Here are some main reasons why receiving help from these people is valuable:

1. Emotional Support: Family, friends, and coworkers may give emotional support during hard times. They give a listening ear, compassion, and empathy, which may help ease stress and feelings of loneliness.

2. Encouragement and inspiration: Supportive folks may give encouragement and inspiration when we confront hurdles or feel disheartened. Their conviction in our

skills may increase self-confidence and resilience.

3. Practical Assistance: Family, friends, and coworkers may provide a helpful hand in practical things, such as running errands, aiding with duties, or giving resources.

4. other viewpoints: Seeking help from others exposes us to other viewpoints and thoughts. This may lead to innovative problem-solving and broader ways of thinking.

5. Feedback and Constructive Criticism: Trusted persons may give constructive feedback and criticism as required. This helps us identify opportunities for development and growth.

6. Social Connection: Interacting with family, friends, and coworkers develops a feeling of belonging and social connection, which is crucial for mental and emotional well-being.

7. Stress Reduction: Sharing our worries with helpful persons may alleviate stress and bring a feeling of relaxation, knowing that we are not alone in our challenges.

8. Coping with obstacles: through difficult times, having a support system may assist in coping with life's obstacles, giving a safety net through stressful conditions.

9. Celebrating Achievements: Family, friends, and coworkers may celebrate our victories and successes with us, making the trip more meaningful and pleasurable.

10. Learning and development: Supportive partnerships create possibilities for learning, self-discovery, and personal development.

11. Increased Resilience: Having a solid support system may boost our capacity to bounce back from setbacks and deal with adversity efficiently.

12. Work-Life Balance: Support from colleagues may help to a healthy work environment and greater work-life balance.

13. Health Benefits: Studies have demonstrated that social support is related to better physical and mental health outcomes.

14. enhanced Happiness: Meaningful interactions with people bring enhanced sentiments of happiness and life satisfaction.

In conclusion, requesting assistance from family, friends, and coworkers is not a sign of weakness but rather a strength. It promotes our well-being, helps us handle problems, and enriches our lives. Cultivating and sustaining these supportive connections is a vital investment in our personal and professional progress.

Join support groups or treatment sessions for persons with ADHD.

Joining support groups or attending therapy sessions particularly geared for those with ADHD may be immensely effective in managing the obstacles that come with the illness. Here are some reasons why participation in these groups or sessions might be valuable:

1. Shared Understanding: Support groups and therapy sessions offer a secure area where persons with ADHD may connect with others who have similar experiences and struggles. This sense of understanding and approval may be reassuring and alleviate feelings of loneliness.

2. Exchange of Coping skills: Members of support groups typically discuss practical coping skills that have worked for them. Learning from others' experiences may

bring fresh ideas and techniques to controlling ADHD symptoms.

3. Emotional Support: Support groups provide a friendly setting where people may discuss their experiences and emotions associated with ADHD without judgment. This emotional support may be crucial for emotional well-being.

4. knowledge and Information: Support groups and therapy sessions may give essential knowledge about ADHD, including its symptoms, treatments, and techniques for managing symptoms successfully.

5. Skill Development: treatment sessions, especially Cognitive-Behavioral Therapy (CBT) or ADHD-specific treatment, may offer practical skills for managing time, increasing organization, and coping with emotional issues.

6. responsibility: Being part of a support group or therapy session creates a feeling of responsibility to focus on personal objectives and self-improvement.

7. Improved Self-Awareness: Group talks and therapy sessions may help people acquire insights into their own habits, strengths, and areas for progress.

8. Peer criticism: Members may give constructive criticism and viewpoints to assist others obtain clarity and fresh methods for managing their ADHD.

9. Reduced Stigma: Being part of a supportive group helps decrease the stigma around ADHD and develop a feeling of acceptance and understanding.

10. Empowerment: Participation in support groups and counseling may empower people to take ownership of their ADHD treatment and general well-being.

11. Enhanced Coping Skills: Through group discussions and treatment, people may develop adaptive strategies to deal with ADHD-related issues, lowering stress and boosting functioning.

12. Networking and Social Connection: Support groups give the opportunity to meet new acquaintances, extend social networks, and establish meaningful relationships with individuals who share shared experiences.

13. Reduced emotions of Loneliness: Connecting with people who endure similar struggles may relieve emotions of loneliness and develop a sense of belonging.

Whether joining an in-person or online support group or attending individual treatment sessions, these possibilities may be crucial in boosting the quality of life for those with ADHD. It's crucial to locate a group or therapist that corresponds with your needs and interests to make the most of these excellent tools.

Educate people about ADHD and lobby for understanding and accommodation.

Educating people about ADHD and pushing for understanding and accommodation is crucial for building a more inclusive and supportive environment for those with ADHD. Here are some things you may take to successfully educate and advocate for ADHD:

Know the Facts: Educate yourself on ADHD, its symptoms, problems, and accessible therapies. Understanding the situation completely can help you convey its effect correctly.

Share your own experiences: Consider sharing your own experiences with ADHD, if you feel comfortable doing so. Personal tales may be great tools for raising awareness and creating empathy.

Use Reliable Resources: Share information from reliable sources, such as medical organizations, research articles, and acknowledged specialists in the area of ADHD.

Raise Awareness: Use social media, blog articles, or local events to promote awareness of ADHD and its effect on persons' lives.

Advocate in the Workplace: If you have ADHD and have issues at work, consider asking for adjustments that will help you flourish. Talk to your company or HR department about possible improvements that might help your productivity.

Support Groups: Encourage the development of support groups in your neighborhood, business, or school to create a safe environment for those with ADHD to share experiences and support one another.

School Advocacy: Advocate for increased understanding of ADHD in schools. Work with teachers, school administrators, and special education personnel to ensure that appropriate accommodations and assistance are given to kids with ADHD.

Training for Educators: Encourage training sessions for educators and school employees on ADHD awareness and techniques for successfully assisting kids with ADHD.

Talk About Accommodations: Share information about the accommodations that may help persons with ADHD, such as additional time for tests, preferred seating, or access to fidget tools.

Address misunderstandings: Address misunderstandings or preconceptions regarding ADHD and encourage awareness that it is a neurological disorder, not a consequence of laziness or lack of discipline.

Support ADHD Advocacy Groups: Get involved with local or national ADHD advocacy groups that aim to improve awareness and understanding of the illness.

Collaborate with Healthcare experts: Work with healthcare experts to provide educational materials or seminars that encourage ADHD awareness.

Be Patient and Empathetic: When teaching people about ADHD, approach the matter with compassion and empathy. Remember that not everyone may have a strong awareness of the disease, and it could take time to correct preconceptions.

Celebrate Neurodiversity: Advocate for an inclusive strategy that celebrates neurodiversity and respects the strengths and skills of persons with ADHD.

By implementing these measures, you may assist in enhancing awareness and empathy for ADHD, eliminate stigma, and create a more friendly and accommodating environment for persons with ADHD in numerous contexts, including schools, workplaces, and communities. Your actions can make a major impact in improving the lives of persons afflicted with ADHD.

CONCLUSION

10 Things I Wish the World Knew About ADHD

1. My ADHD is a Superpower, and It's Bigger Than Any Box You Try to Put Me In "For every weakness I have with executive function, I also have strength. I may be late to meetings or interviews, but I'm constantly trying, sometimes suffering, and many times succeeding in my continual endeavor to satisfy your needs and build my position in this world. I'm still an asset to you because I bring with me heart, resilience, hard work, and a tremendous will to accomplish the impossible. And I won't give up."

Stop seeing yourself as damaged, my companions with ADHD, and start realizing that you have an unstoppable superpower thanks to your attention deficit disease. You may give something new to the world through your unusual enthusiasm, follow-through, and delight in pursuing something which does keep your attention. You are a talented aberration, not a labeled sickness. You cannot sleepwalk through an inauthentic existence. You were born to soar. And if you can live each day with joy and self-love, at the end of your life you will know you lived your life – and not that of someone else.``

2. My ADHD Symptoms Are Invisible... Aside from Knowing Where to Look

You can't determine someone'sreally' ADHD based just on their outward signs of the disorder. I don't appear to struggle to sit still, I don't fidget much outwardly, and I don't get up and walk about when I shouldn't – but that's because my social anxiety makes me frightened to do anything that would be out of sync with the people around me. So I hide my fidgeting and restlessness (in public, anyhow), and I've had people respond with astonishment when I speak about my diagnosis because 'I've never seen you being hyper or fidgety or anything!' Well, no, since I'm investing a big portion of my energy trying to suppress it. Just because you don't notice the symptoms, doesn't imply they aren't there. Some of us merely have to learn to disguise them in order to make it in a neurotypical world."

"I wish people could distinguish between the person I am and the person who has ADHD. They should be able to see how hard I work. I wish I could really clearly comprehend it myself because sometimes I recognize it and sometimes I don't. Please, world, learn what is already known about ADHD, and attempt to encourage and aid people who bear it on their shoulders, like a heavy, invisible cloak. Please realize that beneath those invisible cloaks exist uncommon, unique, brilliant, creative, talented, constructive, but different individuals. Can you see them? Can you see the cloak?"

3. Self-esteem is negatively impacted by ADHD, which worsens the condition and further lowers it.

"A lifetime of missed opportunities, bad social skills, bad first impressions, being too loud, too annoying, too honest, and just being too much has left me with shattered hope, broken dreams, and a lack of confidence," the speaker said. and a broken heart. I have realized that I am faulty – a nasty person. That I am always going to be on the outside looking in. That I have to simultaneously let all this baggage go, so I can relax, while at the same time remembering it so I don't become sidetracked. That the worry and dread of failing consume most of my attention, thus I am locked in a Catch-22: my attention is destroyed by the fear of my lack of attention."

"ADHD is directly responsible for frustration, suffering, and poor self-esteem. Never achieving neurotypical standards grinds up the emotions of people with ADHD. Overreactions and meltdowns are all part of ADHD, but they are amplified by the emotional suffering that comes from taunting and judgment. Everyone with ADHD needs to feel they are worthwhile, competent and wanted. So all you square pegs quit trying to fit into round holes and start digging out your own square niche."

4. We Really Don't Mean to Cause Offense

"People with ADHD don't mean anything personally. We want to call, write, and meet up, but anything that isn't occurring now is too darn hard to keep track of. We don't want to drop off the face of the Earth, but we simply can't get our darn minds in order long enough to remain on it! In short, world, we don't want to damage you. We don't intend to when we do. And we know that most of the time, you don't want to harm us either. We're sorry if the wires got twisted while attempting to transmit that."

"ADHD doesn't make me uncaring, irrational, or unreliable. I am a mature adult and am capable of evolving through challenging circumstances and becoming stronger in areas of weakness. I realize every day what areas are difficult for me. ADHD makes some tasks tougher, but not impossible. The sheer essence of ADHD magnifies introspection because we are so harsh on ourselves, yet in that introspection, we acquire a wonderful perspective of self-awareness, empathy, and grace. I take delight in the concept that the benefit of being diagnosed would enable me to obtain the knowledge and expertise to assist others."

5. It's Beautiful That My Mind Is Differently Organized

"I'm not impulsive! My mind is always distracted because it is simply attracted to everything and finds beauty everywhere. If you will simply admit it, ADHD has beauty. I wish people knew that rather than being limited by my condition, I am empowered and content to recognize it. I am a better person because I have ADHD. I wish everyone understood how excited I am to see where this journey takes me! I'm not defined by my ADHD, but it also doesn't limit me.

A bit jumbled like a kaleidoscope, an ADHD person's life may also be quite beautiful as they discover their own patterns and unique perspectives on the world.

"I wish that people had a better understanding of ADHD as a legitimate, nonlinear style of thinking. Simply because it differs from how most people think and take in information, ADHD is a defect in the world of linear thinking that neurotypical people live in. Nothing about the US is flawed or degraded. The circumstances we encounter most often are what make us vulnerable.

6. We're Making Every Effort to Improve Our Executive Function

"A youngster who is agitated and fidgety in their seat is not always a sign of ADHD. Sometimes it entails feeling completely overwhelmed by the world around you and everything that has to be accomplished within it, as well as a failure since it seems like everyone else can do things that you can't.

"People with ADHD do not intentionally choose to behave badly, forgetful, impulsively, or inefficiently. They usually devised unique coping mechanisms on their own. Imagine you are asked to write your name in cursive using your non-dominant hand and you do not have ADHD. You are asked to move your left foot side to side, move your right foot in circles, and touch your head with your dominant hand all at the same time. not that simple? Much effort is required for someone with ADHD to do tasks that are simple and easy for those without ADHD.

"I'm not late because I don't care; I'm late because I'm either doing something I should have rejected, making a snap decision, or having trouble finding what I need. Being late irritates people with ADHD just as much as it does others who have to wait for them. Please understand that we are doing our best and that we feel terrible about ourselves when we fail.

7. We Are Aware That Our ADHD May Annoy You (So Quit Telling Us That)

Everyone has difficulty with ADHD. It affects instructors, friends, the younger sibling who doesn't know what ADHD is but sees the signs daily, the single mother who is doing her best to help, and the individual themselves. Everyone must learn to deal with it. Work with it and find a way to go around it. ADHD chose us; we didn't select it to be in our lives.

"It's already difficult enough when ADHD prevails. We take it in more than we would admit. Every time our loved ones express those feelings in a similar way by their words, attitudes, or deeds, it validates our embarrassment and displeasure. It is difficult enough to experience them without having them reinforced externally by the reactions of our loved ones. The more our loved ones criticize us, the more we hear their voices in our own self-rebuke. Even after you leave the poisoned area, you may still have emotional reactions. We are always working to fix our mistakes in replay mode, including the social feedback and effects, in order to prevent making the same mistake again. So just let the criticism go. You cannot claim ownership of our ADD moments.

8. Negative feedback may be devastating, especially when we're making an effort.

You have no idea how damaging comments like "You seem distracted" or "You're kind of all over the place" may make us feel, especially when we're already on medication. I want to respond, "I AM calm, I AM focused. One day, I'll show you I'm distracted by reporting to work without taking my medication." You may as well say, "Don't even attempt; your best isn't good enough.

"Those of us who help persons with ADHD or who have the condition themselves are trying our best. To really understand how tiresome ADHD can be and how it affects almost everything, I wish the world could temporarily step into our shoes. Everyone struggles with something, and ADHD (regardless of whether you are the patient or the caregiver) is our issue. I wish the world were more tolerant and understanding in general. Be impartial. No matter who they are, what their circumstances, or whatever their problem may be, be accepting and tolerant of them all.

9. It's Beneficial to Ignore My ADHD.

No amount of scaring, pleading, or counseling is going to make me round, the speaker said. "I've felt like a square peg in a round hole my entire life." It doesn't mean I'm stupid if I make a poor decision. It does not mean I am lazy if I seem disorganized. It doesn't mean that I'm rude if I'm late. I wish people would understand that, despite the fact that my expression gives the impression that I've "checked out," I'm really processing around ten things at once and I'll be right back. I wish people could see how intelligent I really am and how if they could only peek into my head and world for a moment, I could contribute much to both work and relationships.

"I am worth whatever issue my ADHD brain might produce, and I can astound you with a little understanding and patience. Because of ADHD, we operate differently than the majority of successful people, but just because our tactics are odd and you don't understand them doesn't mean they're bad. Do not undervalue me. Don't tie my hands down with insignificant rules or pointless restrictions. Allow me to think and create outside of your little, restrictive box. Sometimes my work defies classification. It exceeds the size of your box.

10. Toward a Future That Is Neurodiverse

"The number of neurodiverse persons is increasing. We don't think of ourselves as being sick, defective, foolish, dysfunctional, lazy, mad, unlovable, inept, or lacking in whatever to offer. We are gifted, kind, and intelligent people who live in a culture that views diversity as undesirable. Although this is difficult, we neither need nor desire pity. We are not challenges; we just have issues.

We are equal despite our differences. Children who were left-handed were formerly forced to use their right hand instead, which was inaccurate, stupid, and harmful. Perhaps a more enlightened era is upon us when people with neurodiversity will be no more 'strange' than someone who uses their left hand.

"I wish the whole world realized what it means to embrace neurodiversity, tolerate our shortcomings, and value our gifts. Although changing procedures and settings to account for such differences may seem like a hassle, adjustments benefit everyone with both temporary and permanent limitations. The creation of check-ins and aiding in task prioritization are essential for the performance of ADHD workers, and those same ADHD changes may assist other employees to stay on track and feel valued. Single parents who struggle to get up in the morning might benefit from flexible schedules to assist those with ADHD. A rising tide will lift all boats if it is used to establish institutions, workplaces, and residences where everyone may succeed.

12 tips for supporting colleagues with ADHD

Individuals with ADHD generally exhibit tremendous drive and are able to hyperfocus on things that are motivated by their passions. They're frequently innovative, able to think holistically and make terrific leaders because of their perseverance. With these abilities, persons with ADHD make a tremendous addition to any workforce. They flourish best in surroundings that play to their talents and support whatever limitations they may have. Such issues might include trouble sustaining attention, impulse, and concentration.

To assist you in supporting a colleague or employee with ADHD, we asked ADHD coaches, business leaders, and individuals with lived experience of ADHD for their suggestions. Here are 12 recommendations to assist you encourage workers with ADHD to perform their jobs and feel welcomed in the work environment.

1. Schedule regular check-ins

When a coworker has ADHD, it is crucial to recognize that they have every intention of getting things done in a timely manner; nevertheless, there are occasionally a few barriers that could be getting in their way. The notion of time is frequently a struggle for someone with ADHD, which cannot only impair the individual's perspective of how long something will take but may also lead them to miscalculate the amount of time before a deadline.

That being said, these coworkers will be effective when they have tight deadlines and are able to consult with someone on how long specific activities could take. Individuals with ADHD can greatly benefit from the routine of regularly scheduled check-ins to help keep them on track and to hold them responsible. Without these human connections, people can unknowingly forget about a detail or a promise. Nonetheless, if a structure is in place, your colleague with ADHD will most certainly be more effective.

2. Make it clear to group members what the immediate goals are.

I'm great at contributing while working with others, but only after we've spoken about what we'll all be doing. I need goals with strict deadlines. I often forget or become sidetracked by other tasks if the deadline is too close. I can usually finish a project before the next meeting if we've spoken as a group and divided it into weekly tasks!

3. Support time management of activities and projects

Those with ADHD may be challenged with time blindness, short attention spans, and planning owing to impaired Executive Function. If your colleague or employee has

ADHD, they might perhaps get stuck with finishing jobs or projects on schedule.

Be proactive to assist them. This might include: Confirm with an email stating tasks or projects with a timeline of when to be finished; emphasize with bullet points what you need from them, why, and the intended result; set up calendar invitations to discuss, with a reminder 24 hours ahead and a 1hr before.

4. Be sympathetic and open-minded

There is just one good approach that can help a colleague or coworker with ADHD. It requires time and patience and sensitivity and it is founded on trust and confidence and open-mindedness. You have to get to know them as a person. Together you have to study, comprehend and recognize their ADHD features and embrace them. Together you have to investigate their experiences and figure out what works and what does not. And you have to be consistently constant and non-judgmental, in the manner that a good friend is.

5. Provide useful strategies to accomplish deadlines

If you have a co-worker or employee with ADHD, you may have observed they have problems meeting deadlines. To encourage their success, they utilize a big wall-mounted calendar or whiteboard positioned on an uncluttered wall area, to record project milestones and due dates. It might also be useful to utilize a visual or aural reminder, to periodically assess milestones and due date progress. Using a color-coded system to notate milestones and due dates may further increase efficacy. It's not unusual for strategies to lose efficacy with time, so if this happens, advise them to develop a new color-coding scheme or shift the placement of the calendar or whiteboard.

6. Help them get things done their way

Focus on the outcome, not the process, and enable us to get there our way. Rewards and penalties seldom work for ADHDers, yet we may accomplish remarkable things when engaged with our interests and beliefs. ADHD paralysis tends to be exacerbated when under pressure, feeling confined/restricted, or in a negative mentality. Allow liberty as much as possible and keep everything focused on achievement.

Encourage folks to get up and move about in meetings or use fidget toys if it helps them to pay attention and have someone summarize and check action items at the conclusion. Be patient with occasional interruptions, it implies we are passionate and interested in the issue.

7. Assign a task buddy to help get work done

Getting started with chores is sometimes the most difficult for individuals with ADHD. They could have emotions of overwhelm or go into 'hyper-focus' with preparing the job but then are too mentally weary to get the work done. Working with an accountability partner or task buddy may be quite useful. Setting objectives with your spouse, and having occasional check-ins give the accountability required to encourage and keep on track.

8. Assist by offering to swap jobs periodically

Unless the ADHD employee has officially declared his/her condition, but you "suspect" a diagnosis is probable. An understanding and sympathetic coworker may make all the difference to someone with ADHD. ADHD folks frequently feel degraded when they make errors. If errors are made often, it may be the individual would flourish better carrying out different jobs. You might aid by possibly asking if he/she would want to exchange responsibilities on occasion. It might also be good to urge him/her to get treatment through an ADHD Coach or

ADHD Career Coach. Try to exhibit empathy and patience. The consequences of feeling overloaded on the job for ADHD individuals may be catastrophic.

9. Discover a few methods to get them going.

Starting a task or attempt might be really tough when you have ADHD. There is more to it than what would first seem to be laziness, purposeful procrastination, or a lack of effort, attention, motivation, or interest (although occasionally that is what it is). Executive functions such as activation and the act of beginning a task are typically impaired in people with ADHD, sometimes to the point of paralysis.

However, there is a lot you can do to assist: Find out whether they are aware of the project's phases, activities, priorities, and expected outputs. Do they want to speak it through (by externalizing or internalizing)?

Encourage them to: take a break to calm their nerves (exercise, drink, fresh air); resolve to work for just 10 minutes (seems less overwhelming); Create a mental map instead of worrying about beginning with a logical presentation; use a countdown timer to "see" the passing of time; and make the exercise game-like ("How many ideas can you come up with in 5 minutes?").

10. Allow them to choose their own approach.

Establish the goal and deadlines for each task, project, or procedure while allowing as much latitude as possible for how the activity is carried out. They are able to participate in the process and use strategies that may appear unorthodox at first, but work to their advantage since they have the freedom to decide how the job is handled and completed. Increased confidence and feelings of accomplishment result from enabling individuals to express their thoughts and providing them with resources.

11. Establish appropriate schedules for everyone.

Asking a colleague with ADHD what time frame makes sense for them to provide you with what you need might be helpful if you require anything from them. Once this has been decided upon, you may need to politely check in with them a few days before the deadline to ensure that it is placed at the top of their list. Furthermore, avoid criticizing them or taking it personally if they don't respond right away since they can become distracted or wait until the last minute to complete tasks. Be positive in all your encounters and consider how they might best help you achieve what you need quickly.

12. Hire an ADHD Coach for support

The greatest method to help a person with ADHD fine-tune job performance is via coaching. Goals will be created and the Coach will assist the Employee increase awareness, and implement methods, systems, or routines to enhance or eliminate performance gaps. They will also discover techniques to increase focus, gain new skills unique to their work and find any applicable abilities that might assist their Employer.

Having an Accountability Partner enhances performance, reinforces newly taught abilities, and trains the workers to advocate for themselves! Seeking and applying this assistance not only leads to enhanced confidence and professional achievement but also makes the Employee more inclined to remain in that capacity owing to work happiness. A win-win scenario!

In conclusion, maintaining Attention Deficit Disorder (ADHD) as an adult involves a diverse strategy that covers numerous facets of life. Through this book, we have studied useful tactics and ways to enable persons with ADHD to take charge of their life and flourish.

Recognizing strengths and appreciating individuality is a vital pillar in this path. By acknowledging and enjoying their strengths, persons with ADHD may acquire confidence, resilience, and a good self-image. Simultaneously, admitting issues with self-compassion enables for successful problem-solving and progress.

Time management, organization, and routine formation are the backbone of good ADHD control. Implementing practical tools, such as planners, reminders, and routines, creates organization and limits unwanted distractions, increasing attention and productivity.

Mindfulness and meditation activities have a significant role in relaxing a hyperactive mind, lowering stress, and enhancing concentration. By increasing present-moment awareness, persons with

ADHD may boost their ability to focus and regulate emotions successfully.

Engaging in regular exercise, having a balanced diet, and getting adequate sleep are not only vital for general health but also have a favorable influence on treating ADHD symptoms.

Seeking help from healthcare experts, joining support groups, or attending therapy sessions provide significant resources for understanding, managing, and living with ADHD. The affirmation, direction, and empathy obtained from these sources lead to enhanced well-being and a feeling of belonging.

Advocating for understanding and accommodation is a key step toward building a more inclusive and supportive workplace for those with ADHD. Educating people about ADHD helps decrease stigma and increases empathy, producing a more sympathetic and caring society.

Ultimately, conquering adult ADHD is a continuous adventure that demands patience, self-awareness, and a commitment to improvement. By applying the tactics given in this book and relying on available resources, persons with ADHD may negotiate life's problems with fortitude and embrace their full potential. With determination and assistance, people may construct a meaningful path toward success, happiness, and general well-being. Remember, you are not defined by your ADHD; you are empowered to design your narrative and make the most of your unique skills.